The • Life Cycle • Series

The Life Cycle of a

POLAR BEAR

Rebecca Sjonger & Bobbie Kalman

Crabtree Publishing Company

www.crabtreebooks.com

The Life Cycle Series

A Bobbie Kalman Book

Dedicated by Rebecca Sjonger
To my little cub, Jane Catherine Sjonger Miller

Editor-in-Chief
Bobbie Kalman

Writing team
Rebecca Sjonger
Bobbie Kalman

Substantive editors
Amanda Bishop
Kelley MacAulay

Project editor
Robin Johnson

Editors
Molly Aloian
Kathryn Smithyman

Design
Margaret Amy Salter
Samantha Crabtree (cover)

Production coordinator
Heather Fitzpatrick

Photo research
Crystal Foxton

Consultant
Patricia Loesche, Ph.D., Animal Behavior Program,
Department of Psychology, University of Washington

Illustrations
Barbara Bedell: page 5 (brown bear)
Barb Hinterhoeller: page 20
Bonna Rouse: back cover, pages 10, 11 (all except top), 16
Margaret Amy Salter: pages 5 (sun bear & black bear), 11 (top)

Photographs
Bryan & Cherry Alexander/Photo Researchers, Inc.: page 12
© Tom Walker/Visuals Unlimited: page 24
Other images by Corbis, Corel, Creatas, Digital Vision, and Photodisc

Crabtree Publishing Company

www.crabtreebooks.com   1-800-387-7650

Copyright © **2006 CRABTREE PUBLISHING COMPANY**.
All rights reserved. No part of this publication may be reproduced,
stored in a retrieval system or be transmitted in any form or by any
means, electronic, mechanical, photocopying, recording, or otherwise,
without the prior written permission of Crabtree Publishing Company.
In Canada: We acknowledge the financial support of the Government of
Canada through the Book Publishing Industry Development Program
(BPIDP) for our publishing activities.

Cataloging-in-Publication Data
Sjonger, Rebecca.
The life cycle of a polar bear / Rebecca Sjonger & Bobbie Kalman.
    p. cm. -- (The life cycle series)
Includes index.
ISBN-13: 978-0-7787-0668-7 (rlb)
ISBN-10: 0-7787-0668-0 (rlb)
ISBN-13: 978-0-7787-0698-4 (pbk)
ISBN-10: 0-7787-0698-2 (pbk)
1. Polar bear--Life cycles--Juvenile literature. I. Kalman, Bobbie. II. Title.
QL737.C27S57 2005
599.786--dc22
                                    2005020743
                                    LC

**Published in
the United States**
PMB16A
350 Fifth Ave.
Suite 3308
New York, NY
10118

**Published
in Canada**
616 Welland Ave.,
St. Catharines, Ontario
Canada
L2M 5V6

**Published in the
United Kingdom**
73 Lime Walk
Headington
Oxford
OX3 7AD
United Kingdom

**Published
in Australia**
386 Mt. Alexander Rd.,
Ascot Vale (Melbourne)
VIC 3032

Contents

Polar bears are mammals

A polar bear is a **mammal**. A mammal is a **warm-blooded** animal. The body of a warm-blooded animal stays about the same temperature in both hot and cold places.

A mammal has body parts called lungs for breathing air. It also has a backbone. A mammal's body is covered in hair or fur. A baby mammal **nurses**, or drinks milk from its mother's body.

4

Bears of the sea

Polar bears are **marine mammals**. Marine mammals live mainly in oceans. Scientists call polar bears *Ursus maritimus*, or "bears of the sea." Unlike some marine mammals, however, polar bears are equally comfortable living in water and on land. They are often considered to be both marine mammals and land animals.

Polar bears are excellent swimmers and divers. A polar bear can hold its breath for over one minute under water.

The bear family

Polar bears are members of the bear family. There are eight **species**, or types, of bears. They include brown bears, sun bears, and American black bears. Polar bears are the largest species of bear. In fact, polar bears are the largest meat-eating animals that live on land!

Brown bears are closely related to polar bears.

There are more American black bears than there are any other bear species in the world.

Sun bears are the smallest bears.

5

Where do polar bears live?

A polar bear's **habitat** is the Arctic. A habitat is the natural place where an animal lives. All polar bears live in the **North Polar Region**, or the area surrounding the North Pole. The North Polar Region includes the Arctic Ocean and the northern **coasts** of North America, Europe, and Asia. Most polar bears live on ice along the coasts and near the many islands in the Arctic Ocean.

Chilling in the Arctic

The **climate** in the Arctic is cold, dry, and windy. Some parts of the Arctic are covered with snow and ice year round. In winter, the temperature can drop below -22° F (-30° C). Even in the middle of summer, temperatures rarely rise above 50° F (10° C)!

On thick ice

Most polar bears live and hunt on **pack ice**. Pack ice is huge, thick pieces of ice that float in the Arctic Ocean. Pack ice forms when **ice floes**, or flat sheets of ice, freeze together. Pack ice is usually about ten feet (3 m) thick. It is strong enough to hold the weight of polar bears, as well as many other arctic animals!

Summer meltdown

Many polar bears live in southern regions of the Arctic. In these areas, the pack ice melts in summer. Pack ice melts slowly, so polar bears stay on it for as long as they can. In places where the ice melts completely, polar bears move onto land for the summer. The polar bear, shown above, is spending its summer on land.

7

A polar bear's body

A polar bear can stay warm even on the icy lands and in the freezing waters of the Arctic. It stays warm because its body is designed to survive in this habitat. A polar bear's body can **conserve**, or hold in, a lot of heat. In fact, a polar bear may actually become too hot when it moves quickly!

A polar bear has a keen sense of smell. It uses its sense of smell to find food hidden under snow.

A polar bear uses its sharp teeth to tear into food.

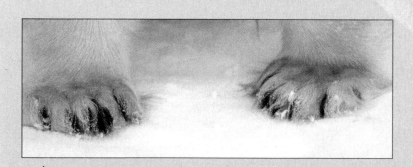

Paws and claws

A polar bear has large paws. The toes on a polar bear's front paws are partly **webbed**, or connected by flaps of skin. The powerful paws and webbed toes act as paddles that pull the polar bear's big body through water. When a polar bear walks on pack ice, it grips the slippery surface using its strong, pointed claws.

Holding in heat

A polar bear's body holds in heat in many ways. A polar bear has white fur all over its body. The fur is made up of several layers. The top layer of fur consists of long **guard hairs**. These hairs keep cold water from reaching the bear's skin. Beneath the guard hairs is a layer of fur called **underfur**. Underfur traps heat close to the polar bear's skin. The skin is black. The color black absorbs the sun's heat. Beneath the bear's skin is a thick layer of fat called **blubber**. Blubber helps hold in the bear's body heat.

A polar bear has small bumps on the soles of its paws. The bumps grip slippery ice. The soles of the bear's paws are also furry. The fur keeps the bear's feet warm.

9

Every animal goes through a set of changes called a **life cycle**. First, the animal is born or hatches from an egg. It then grows, and its body changes. Finally, the animal becomes **mature**, or adult. Mature animals can **mate**, or join together with other animals of their species to make babies.

Life span

A life cycle is not the same as a **life span**. An animal's life span is the length of time the animal lives. In the wild, male polar bears live for about 25 years, and female polar bears live for about 30 years. Polar bears kept in zoos can live for over 40 years. Their lives can never be the same as the lives of polar bears in the wild, however.

A polar bear's life cycle

A polar bear's life cycle begins with the birth of a **cub**, or baby polar bear. Cubs are born in groups called **litters**. Most litters consist of only two cubs. A mother polar bear feeds and protects her cubs. When the cubs are about three months old, their mother begins teaching them how to hunt and swim.

By the time most polar bears are two or three years old, they are ready to leave their mothers and live on their own. They are not yet mature, however. Female polar bears are mature when they are about five years old. Male polar bears are mature when they are about six years old.

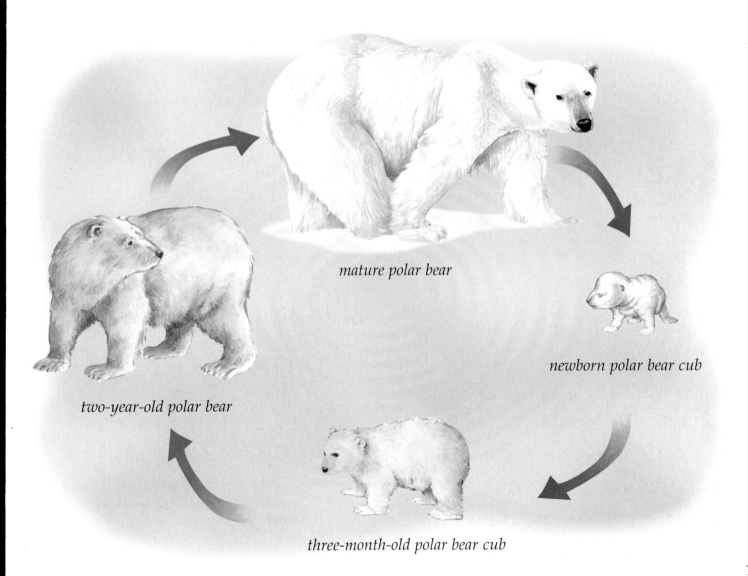

mature polar bear

newborn polar bear cub

two-year-old polar bear

three-month-old polar bear cub

Newborn cubs

Newborn polar bear cubs weigh only about one pound (0.5 kg) each! Cubs cannot see or hear. Their eyes and ears are sealed shut. Their tiny bodies appear to be furless, but they have fine, short hairs covering their skin.

Depending on Mom

Polar bear cubs are totally helpless when they are born. Their mother must feed and protect them. The cubs nurse from their mother's body. For the first few weeks of their lives, the cubs do nothing but nurse and nestle close to their mother to keep warm. The cubs, shown left, are nursing.

Time to explore

When the cubs are about four weeks old, their ears open and they can hear. About one week later, their eyes open and they can see. By the time the cubs are two months old, they begin exploring their **den**. The cubs also begin to wrestle and play together.

Hello world!

By the time the cubs are about three months old, they have gained over 20 pounds (9 kg) and have grown thick fur. They are now ready to leave their den. The cubs follow their mother out into the chilly air. It is time for them to learn about life in the Arctic.

These polar bear cubs are ready to explore the world outside their den.

13

Growing up

When cubs leave their den, they stay close to their mother. Their mother teaches them how to survive in the Arctic. Over the next few years, the cubs will learn important skills from her, such as swimming and hunting. The mother bear may do these activities more often than she needs to in order to let her cubs practice.

On guard

The mother bear works hard to protect her cubs from danger. Male polar bears may attack and eat the cubs if they can get close enough to them. The mother will fight males that are much larger than she is to save her cubs from harm.

A mother polar bear is always alert. She watches over her cubs as they play.

Practice fighting

Polar bear cubs born in the same litter are great playmates! They wrestle, play fight, and chase one another. Their mother allows them to practice fighting this way. Someday the cubs will need to know how to defend themselves, so the time spent wrestling with **siblings** is good preparation!

Leaving Mom

Most polar bears are **weaned** when they are two-and-a-half years old. Although they are not yet fully grown, the young polar bears have already learned how to hunt. Many polar bears leave their mothers at this age. The bears set out on their own to find food. In places where food is hard to find, however, they may stay with their mothers for up to two more years.

Adult polar bears

Adult polar bears are **solitary** animals. Solitary animals live alone. Polar bears hunt, feed, and sleep by themselves. When two polar bears meet in the wild, the larger bear stays where it is and the smaller bear runs away. Adult males and females come together only to mate.

Sleepy bears

Adult polar bears spend two-thirds of their lives resting. They need to rest to keep up their strength! Polar bears use a lot of energy walking, swimming, hunting for **prey**, and eating. Prey are the animals the polar bears hunt and eat.

Fully grown polar bears

Fully grown male polar bears are twice as big as fully grown female polar bears. Male polar bears are not fully grown until they are about fourteen years of age. They are over eight feet (2.4 m) in length from the tips of their noses to the tips of their tails. They weigh between 650 and 1,750 pounds (295-794 kg)! Female polar bears are fully grown by the time they reach age five or six. They are just under six-and-a-half feet (2 m) long, and they weigh between 330 and 770 pounds (150-349 kg).

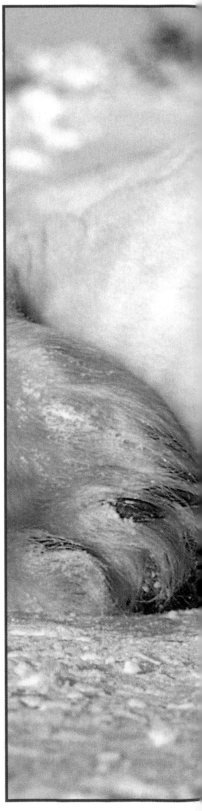

16

Mating season

The time of year during which polar bears mate is called their **mating season**. Polar bears mate only in spring. Each spring, there are fewer female polar bears that are ready to mate than there are male polar bears. There are fewer females because female polar bears do not mate while they are raising their cubs. Since there are more male polar bears than there are females, the males fight one another for chances to mate with the females. When a male and a female pair up to mate, they stay together for several days. The male then leaves. Male polar bears do not help raise the cubs.

Pregnancy on pause

After a male polar bear and a female polar bear mate, the female becomes **pregnant**. A pregnant female has one or more **embryos**, or developing babies, inside her body. Polar bear embryos do not begin growing right away, however. They begin to grow in autumn.

The female bear must eat a lot of food for the embryos to grow. In the Arctic, there is little food for the female to eat in spring and summer. In autumn, however, there is food available for her to eat, so the embryos can begin to grow. The embryos then **gestate**, or develop inside the mother's body, for about two months.

A mother polar bear may carry an embryo in her body for up to 250 days before it begins to grow into a cub.

Ready for the cubs

When a female polar bear is ready to give birth to her cubs, she makes a cozy den. The den is a safe, warm place that is protected from the harsh arctic winter. Most females make their dens on land, close to coasts. Other females build their dens in the snow that covers pack ice. A female builds her den by tunneling through icy snow or frozen **peat**. She then carves out a cave at the end of the tunnel. In mid winter, the mother gives birth inside the den she has made.

Inside this polar bear den, the cubs play together while their mother rests. The cubs will wake their mother when they are hungry and want to nurse.

A cub is born

The first few times a female polar bear gives birth, she will likely have only one cub. After she has given birth a few times, the female may give birth to a litter of up to four cubs. Most female polar bears have two cubs in their litters, however. Later in her life, the female will have smaller litters, until she once again gives birth to only one cub at a time.

*When only one or two polar bear cubs are born in a litter, there is a greater chance that the cubs will survive. The mother bear can give both cubs the care and protection that they need. This mother bear is watching for **predators** while her cub sleeps.*

On the hunt

Polar bears spend the winter hunting for food on pack ice. They are **carnivores**, or animals that eat other animals. Polar bears hunt and eat animals such as walruses, narwhals, beluga whales, and many types of seals. They also eat smaller animals such as sea birds and their eggs. Most polar bears use a method of hunting called **still-hunting**.

To still-hunt, a polar bear sits silently on pack ice for hours and waits for prey to appear at a **breathing hole**. A breathing hole is an opening in the ice. It is used by mammals that live in water, when they need to breathe air. When prey comes up for air, the waiting polar bear grabs it.

Polar bears are excellent hunters. The polar bear shown above is still-hunting at a breathing hole.

Silent stalkers

A polar bear sometimes walks or swims long distances in search of food. It may also **stalk**, or silently follow, its prey. Despite its large size, a polar bear can creep up on other animals because its white fur blends in with ice and snow. A polar bear also swims under water to get close to prey sitting on ice. Then it leaps out of the water in a surprise attack!

Eat and run

As soon as a polar bear finds its prey, it attacks! One blow from a polar bear's powerful paw is enough to kill most animals. The polar bear quickly eats its prey's skin and fat. These parts have important **nutrients**, which the polar bear needs to stay healthy. The polar bear does not save what it has not eaten. Other animals finish the leftovers.

A polar bear may swim over 62 miles (100 km) to find food!

23

Feasting and fasting

Polar bears eat many animals during autumn, winter, and early spring. The bears eat the fat from the bodies of their prey. Eating a lot of fat is good for polar bears! The fatty foods add blubber to their bodies.

Blubber helps keep polar bears warm. In summer, when some polar bears are trapped on land, they may eat plant foods such as grass and berries. Polar bears also eat **carrion**. Carrion is the flesh of dead animals.

A polar bear can eat four-and-a-half pounds (2 kg) of fat every day! This polar bear is eating a seal.

24

Summer fast

In summer, when pack ice begins to melt, polar bears cannot always find enough prey. Most polar bears **fast**, or stop eating, during this time. When polar bears are fasting, their bodies use less energy than when they are eating every day. Sometimes the bodies of polar bears use energy so slowly that the bears do not need to eat again for several months!

25

Important arctic animals

Polar bears are important arctic animals. They are the **apex**, or top, predators of the Arctic. Apex predators help keep a healthy balance between predator and prey **populations**. A population is the total number of one species of animal living in a certain area. By hunting many seals and whales, polar bears keep the populations of these animals from growing too large. If there were no polar bears in the Arctic, there could soon be too many seals and whales. These animals would then eat most of the other animals! Before long, many arctic animals could be left with no food to eat.

When polar bears are not sleeping, they are usually eating!

There is plenty of pack ice during cold winter
months, so it is a good time for polar bears to hunt.
This polar bear has just finished eating a seal.

Threats to polar bears

At this time, polar bears are not **endangered**. Endangered animals are at risk of disappearing from Earth. The main reason that they are not endangered is that most polar bears live far away from people. Scientists estimate that 25,000 polar bears live in the Arctic. Polar bears still face many serious threats, however.

Global warming

A serious threat to polar bears is **global warming**, or the rise in the Earth's average temperature. This increase in temperature occurs because **greenhouse gases** are being released into the air. Greenhouse gases trap warm air close to the Earth's surface and make the whole planet slightly warmer.

Melting ice

When the Arctic becomes warmer, pack ice melts earlier in the year. Polar bears have less time to hunt on the ice. This forces them to move onto land, where many polar bears cannot find enough food to eat. The pack ice melts earlier each year, causing more and more polar bears to starve.

About 1,000 polar bears are killed by hunters every year. The laws of some countries allow people to hunt polar bears only for food. In countries without laws, however, too many polar bears are being hunted.

Poisonous pollution

Companies that use **toxic**, or poisonous, chemicals also harm polar bears. The toxic chemicals pollute air and water in the places where they are released. Over time, much of the polluted air and water end up in the Arctic. Water and air pollution can cause many arctic animals to become sick. When polar bears eat these animals, they also become sick.

Collecting oil

Companies that sell **natural resources** such as oil find the resources under ground in the Arctic. The companies set up **mining rigs** to collect the oil. Having mining rigs in the Arctic increases the risk that environmental disasters, such as **oil spills**, will occur there. The noisy rigs also frighten polar bears and other arctic animals.

29

Helping polar bears

Polar bears may live in a habitat that is far from your home, but you can still learn a lot about them without traveling to the Arctic! Set up your own research station at home. Borrow books about polar bears from your local library and research polar bears on the Internet. As you learn, you can tell your friends and family how global warming and pollution are hurting polar bears. The more information you give others about polar bears, the more people will remember to help them.

Polar bear tours

Some people do live in **communities** that are close to polar bear habitats! Many of these people are trying to help polar bears. Tourists often travel to the communities in order to see arctic wildlife such as polar bears. The local people offer tours that the tourists can take to learn more about these beautiful bears. Tourists and local people must take great care not to spoil the habitats of the polar bear, however.

The town of Churchill, Manitoba in Canada is famous for its polar bear tours. The tours bring a lot of money into the community. These tourists are lucky to see a polar bear up close!

31

Glossary

Note: Boldfaced words that are defined in the text may not appear in the glossary.

climate The normal, long-term weather conditions of an area

coast The land next to the sea; also called the seashore

community A group of people who live together in the same place

den A sheltered area where a mother polar bear and her cubs live

greenhouse gas A gas such as carbon dioxide that is in air and which contributes to global warming

mining rig Equipment used to get natural resources out of the ground

natural resource A material found in nature that is necessary or useful to people

nutrient A natural substance that helps animals and plants grow

oil spill Describing a large amount of oil that is dumped into water or onto land

peat A type of damp soil found in the Arctic

predator An animal that hunts and eats other animals

sibling A brother or sister

wean To gradually stop nursing

Index

1 2 3 4 5 6 7 8 9 0   Printed in the U.S.A.   4 3 2 1 0 9 8 7 6 5